Reconnecting to Self:

How to Create a Better Relationship with . . . You!

Susan K. Merrill

Photography By Dave Merrill

Lynn,
Thanks for your
friendship!
Take good care,
Susan
&
Dave

Reconnecting to Self:
How to Create a Better Relationship with . . . You!

Library of Congress Control Number: 2016911951

ISBN: 978-0-692-74929-6 (softbound)
ISBN: 978-0-692-74930-2 (e-book)

Photography by Dave Merrill (www.DaveMerrillPhotography.com)

Design and photo post-production by Magrit Baurecht (www.CoreCreativeTeam.com)

Author photograph by Kat Ly

Edited by Susan Herman

Printed in the United States

www.ReconnectingToSelf.com

Table of Contents

Preface

I know how it feels to lose the important connection with your inner Self. For me, losing the connection didn't happen all at once; rather, it was a slow, almost imperceptible detachment. I was about seven or eight years old when I first became aware that I was living in a home filled with tension. As I got older, I became increasingly sensitive to the negativity clouding the air. My family never underwent a big, life changing event or trauma as happens in some families. But my dad disliked his job, was often angry or upset, and his behavior was unpredictable with us kids. Mom was overwhelmed trying to take care of four children, a big house, yard, garden, laundry, shopping, and working part-time. My brothers often argued or fought. And I felt sad and alone much of the time. Little by little, my Self and I became disconnected from each other.

I developed many coping strategies to help deal with the pain I felt, among them keeping my thoughts and feelings to myself. While this skill functioned as a shield from my family's emotional ups and downs, it also meant that I lost my voice. Not speaking up for myself was the first step in the disconnection process. I also learned to focus on others' needs instead of my own. I learned my needs were not that important. Finally, I learned that if I wanted attention, I should perform well — I tried to be as "perfect" as possible. It's not that anyone told me to do these things, but there was not a welcoming or accepting person available to whom I could talk or express my feelings.

These strategies worked for me in many ways. I did well in school. Being a quiet, people pleaser meant that most teachers and bosses liked me. I had friends. The downside is that, unless I was "perfect" and *everyone* liked me, I felt I didn't have value. I hid how I really felt about things from others and eventually, from myself as well. I never felt good enough. I thought I couldn't possibly be loved for just being me. On the outside I looked fine, but underneath I felt insecure, unsure, and alternately depressed and anxious.

Fast forward through college, jobs, and marriage to the day my son was born. I took one look into his beautiful, blue eyes and fell — totally and completely — in love. While I knew my parents had done the best they could, I was also aware that the kind of parenting I'd received wasn't going to be good enough. I knew that my son deserved a mom who could support him in a way that my mom had not been able to support me. Though I really wasn't sure what that meant or how to do it, I started the process of reconnecting to my inner Self.

Over time, and after one-on-one talk therapy and reading many books, I gained insight into what had gone wrong and how I'd lost my Self. I learned that I have value whether I do everything well or not. This was an especially important lesson to learn when I was going through a divorce. Just because my marriage failed, didn't mean I was a failure. I started making choices that felt good to me and not simply to please everyone else. I found my voice and started on the path to rediscover my Self that continues to this day. My journey toward reconnection has positively affected all areas of my life, not just my parenting skills.

When I looked back at my own healing, I knew I wanted to share the process of self-inquiry and healing with others. I went back to school and received a master's degree in counseling psychology and became a licensed therapist. One of the astonishing things I learned on my healing path and in my practice is that there are *so many people* who struggle with a disconnection from their inner Self. When I started out, I thought it was just me! The stories and circumstances are varied, of course, but so many of us lose this important connection. Let me reassure you, the connection to Self can be repaired! And you can learn to create a better relationship with your Self.

While this book will not answer *all* of your questions about how to reconnect with your Self or replace therapy for those who may need it, my deepest and most sincere hope is that it will help you start on your *own* journey to create a better relationship with your Self. And that as you deepen your connection to Self, you will start to realize and appreciate what an amazing, unique, and one-of-a-kind person you truly are. Enjoy your journey.

Susan

Introduction:
Why Reconnecting to Your Self is Not Selfish

The most important relationship you will ever have is the relationship you have with your Self. And the truth is, many of us have not focused on improving our relationship with ourselves. This seems too self-serving or self-centered. Of course, we need relationships with other people to help us throughout our lives: parents, siblings, friends, lovers, spouses, kids, neighbors, co-workers, and more. Yet the one person in *all* of these relationships is you. *You* are the common denominator in every area of your life.

In our culture, we don't spend much time trying to understand ourselves or to get to know ourselves better. We take exercise classes, continuing education for our careers, and pay for instruction for a better golf swing, but rarely make an investment to simply gain Self knowledge. We surf the internet and social media to see what our friends are doing, but we don't spend time or energy looking up information to help ourselves grow. Sometimes we aren't even aware that we *have* an inner Self with whom we can connect and who can help guide us. We don't know that our connection with this inner Self can be improved upon. When we ignore ourselves and our inner worlds, we become disconnected from our Self.

When our connection with our Self is lost, we feel unsure, insecure, discouraged, anxious, indecisive, depressed, or stuck. We may feel adrift or untethered. We lose the capacity to clearly *know* what we want, need or desire. Sometimes, we tell ourselves this is what being an adult looks like, trudging one foot in front of the other, our days consisting of little fun, little joy, and little sense of purpose. This is the disconnection from Self.

Elsa from the Disney movie *Frozen* is a simple, if dramatic, example of what a disconnected life looks like. At the beginning of the movie, we see that Elsa has an amazing ability to create ice and snow sculptures with her hands. When she accidentally injures her little sister, Anna, she is told she needs to learn to control her gift and to hide it from others. There is no one to teach her *how* to use her talent safely, so she shuts herself away in her room, unhappy, alone, afraid, and isolated.

Disconnection from our inner Self usually happens slowly, over time. When we were born, we had a very clear idea about our needs. Listen to a newborn's insistent cries and you become instantly aware when the baby is unhappy. I'm hungry. I'm tired. My diaper needs to be changed. I want to be held! And even though the baby lacks sophisticated means to communicate, she is *certain* of her needs and has no difficulty letting caregivers know about them. Many of us lose this ability to discern and communicate our needs over time.

In some ways, disconnection makes sense. We are social animals and live with other people who also have needs. Others' needs often conflict with our own. As children, we learn the importance of trying to please our parents. In school we learn to wait our turn and raise our hand. Sports teach us to be team players. As parents, we put our children first. In our jobs we take care of the company's bottom line — working long hours which interferes not only with our families, friends and social life, but also with our individual needs.

Putting others ahead of our ourselves is a valuable skill. But when we *always* put the needs of others first, it becomes reflexive and automatic. We forget about our needs or that we even *have* needs independent from others. When we respond to others first and ignore or temper our own needs for extended periods of time, sadly, we lose ourselves. We disconnect from our inner Self.

Next time you watch the movie *My Big Fat Greek Wedding*, look at Toula's character. At the beginning of the story, she is working in her parent's restaurant. Her family needs her. She dresses in frumpy clothes because she's so busy working at the restaurant she doesn't have time to shop. Who would see her anyway? She doesn't have prospects for a career or romance and she is very unhappy living the life that was chosen for her by her family. Eventually, though, she signs up for a computer class, gets contact lenses and a boyfriend and is off on a new life adventure where *she* is the star in the life she has chosen. Fundamentally, Toula's journey is about the reconnection to Self.

Another contributor in the disconnection process happens when our sense of Self is solely defined by others or outside events. If we allow others to define who we are, how we spend our time, or what is important, our lives feel empty — something is missing. Scattered memories from our childhoods get combined with stories told by our parents, families, and friends. We add in our school experiences, jobs, and relationships and mix these all together to come up with a definition of who we are. We need to question whether the memories and stories are actually a good representation of our past or are how we want to define ourselves. We are not the same person that we were yesterday, let alone who we were twenty years ago. We are *more* than our past experiences, the roles we take on, and the jobs we perform.

We don't spend time, or enough of it anyway, to really figure out who we *were* vs. who we are *now* or who we *want to be going forward*. When we don't define our *own* sense of Self, we are tossed about on the winds of others' conflicting whims and needs. We lose touch with our feelings. Then we find ourselves being emotional about things that, logically, we know shouldn't upset us so much. Or we numb our emotions and don't react when things actually should bother us. We may be aware that changes need to be made in our lives, but just go along without standing up for ourselves. We allow others to treat us in ways that don't feel good, yet we don't set healthy boundaries.

Disconnection from Self also occurs when we are not focused in the present moment. Our minds are already three steps ahead or three steps behind. We are preoccupied about the presentation we have to give at work when we are playing with our kids, or we're stewing about something that happened a couple of days/months/years ago instead of showing up in our lives now. It is impossible to stay connected to Self when our minds are not actually here in the present moment.

And finally, without a secure connection to Self, we forfeit the ability to reach our full potential. The *Star Wars* character, Luke Skywalker, illustrates this concept. When we are first introduced to him, he doesn't know about the "force" already within him or how to connect to his powerful inner Self. Yet with the proper teachers, focus, and practice, connection to Self allows us to show up in our lives so we expand and grow — regardless of whether we ever learn Jedi lightsaber skills.

Connection to our inner Self is so important because this is where our thoughts and feelings, our memories, desires, dreams, beliefs, attitudes, values, and hopes reside. They make up our rich inner world and these attributes are as unique as our fingerprint. When we have a secure bond with our Self, there is an alignment between our thoughts, feelings, and actions that is otherwise missing.

Our inner Self is our compass, giving us guidance and direction. Our Self confidence increases as we start to trust our Self. The decisions we make and actions we take will be congruent, have meaning for us and just plain feel good. There is no one else like you! You are worth *every bit* of effort it takes to create a better connection with your inner Self.

So here is the good news: we can learn to reconnect with our inner Self! It is never too late. By becoming curious about who we are and by wanting to create a better relationship with our inner Self, we start the reconnection process. *Reconnecting to Self* highlights some of the common ways we disconnect from our inner world and how to make positive changes for reconnection. It explores the relationship between our thoughts and feelings and how they impact us and our connection to Self. We learn how to revise thought patterns that are no longer supportive to our well-being and how to make sense of our emotional landscape. We also learn to recognize the cycles, stories, beliefs, and themes that have kept us stuck and explore ways to modify them. And finally, we focus on how to continue to grow our newfound knowledge and connection to Self in the future.

As you read, take time to enjoy the contemplative images and short reflections. The readings are paired with photographs to provide a visually beautiful and peaceful place for inner connection time. They are meant to create a "pause," a relaxing, tranquil, and grounding place to take your mind as you allow the concepts to sink in and carve out some quiet time. Dave, the photographer, writes, "The images in this book are a reminder that the world is much bigger than our habitual thoughts and emotions. Spending time in the natural elements is healing because every cell in our body resonates with earth, water, warmth, color, and spaciousness. While photographs are only a representation of these elements, when used in combination with your awareness, they create positive healing benefits."

One meaningful way to use the photographs in the book is to imagine putting yourself in the picture. Ask yourself, where would I be in this picture and what would I hear, feel and smell if I were actually there? Take a deep breath and relax as you exhale. Continue breathing slowly as you think about the reflections and explore their meaning for you.

I realize the importance of creating a secure connection with my inner Self. As I tune into my inner compass – my thoughts, feelings, memories, desires, dreams, beliefs, attitudes, values, and hopes – I am open to new discoveries about my Self.

The ideas for this book come from the field of psychology. Concepts are included from Emotionally Focused Therapy, Mindfulness, Cognitive Behavioral Therapy, Internal Family Systems, Narrative Therapy, and more. The essence of the various theories are distilled into nuggets of wisdom that can be applied to understanding the important connection to Self.

This book is not a step by step instruction guide, so it will be up to you to identify the concepts that strike a chord with your inner Self. Some suggestions for doing this include:

- Mark the pages that resonate with you and read them over again when you've finished the book to look for the similarities or a theme.

- Keep a journal handy and write about a page or concept that speaks to you.

- Open the book to a random page and absorb its message.

- Skip the text and let the photographic images soothe you.

- Share meaningful insights with a friend or therapist.

- Write a reflection on a sticky note and post it on your car dashboard, bathroom mirror, or another place where it can remind you of its wisdom throughout the day.

You get the idea. Feel free to use this book in a way that feels good to you and supports your journey to reconnect to your inner Self.

I use this book in a way that feels supportive
to my journey and my growth.

Chapter ❶
The Basics of Reconnection

Reconnecting to Self, at its most basic level, is a practice that helps us understand, manage and heal our pain. Practicing reconnection helps us take proactive steps in our lives, not just to prevent further pain, but also to accomplish our goals and realize our dreams. Reconnection takes us on a journey that, while different for each person, follows this general pattern:

- We learn to be present with ourselves and truly embrace the unique and wonderful individuals we are. When we do this, our pain is reduced and we suffer less.

- When we no longer spend so much time managing our pain, we have more energy.

- With more energy, we get to know ourselves even better. This, in turn, leads to Self trust and to increased Self confidence.

- When we have more energy, Self trust and Self confidence, we can creatively try new activities including reaching out to others for support.

- When we have energy, Self trust, Self confidence and caring people to support us, we make choices that ring true with our inner Self. This becomes a foundation from which we can live our lives that is supportive to ourselves and our well-being.

As we create a secure connection to Self, we generate a new and positive inner cycle in our lives. The more we know and trust ourselves, the better decisions we make. When we make better decisions, we feel more positive about ourselves. The more positive we feel about ourselves, the more we attract nurturing and supportive people into our lives. With supportive people in our lives, the more we are able to know and trust ourselves. And around and around we go in this new, healthy cycle.

By reconnecting to my inner Self, I open myself to creating a life that is fulfilling,
meaningful, and satisfying to me. I start on my path
to connect with my inner Self now.

Defining Self

Who exactly is our inner Self? The fields of psychology, mindfulness, philosophy, and religion provide many explanations and ideas. It is beyond the scope of this book to examine these in detail, but take a moment to explore which of the following definitions of Self fits for you:

- It is our true nature, which naturally gravitates toward goodness, love, compassion, and wisdom.
- It is a sense of wholeness.
- It is our wise one or our core being.
- It is part of an all-knowing universe or universal truth.
- It is our God-like nature.
- It is the part of us that strives for the highest and greatest good in our lives.
- It is our soul, with us when we are born, throughout our lives and beyond.
- It is love, our inner essence.
- It is our inner voice.

Feel free to use a description of Self that fits best with your own religious beliefs, personal philosophy, or values. For ease of communication, this book uses the simple word *"Self"* to describe this inner part of you.

I define my inner Self according to my values and beliefs
and in a way that resonates with me.

Getting Started

Reconnecting with our inner Self requires time and practice. Practice means checking in with yourself regularly — every morning, or at the end of the day, after the stressful meeting with your boss, or an argument with your spouse or kids. Think about it. Everything we know how to do, we had to learn and then practice: walking, talking, reading, riding a bike, skiing, and creating spreadsheets on the computer. Connecting to our Self is no different. We need to practice consciously and diligently. Checking in and connecting will get easier and quicker over time, but in the beginning, it will be important to set aside a little time every day for thoughtful reflection.

*I create the time and space needed to connect
with my inner Self daily.*

Curiosity

Becoming curious about your Self is key. Curiosity is not judgmental, critical, or hard-hearted. Curiosity is open and inquisitive. Curiosity couples a desire for knowledge about ourselves with compassion and caring. Not one of us is perfect. Yet, we are all lovable as special, one-of-a-kind individuals. You are the *only* you who will ever exist.

I am open, inquisitive, caring, and curious about myself.
I am unique. I am me.

Focusing Inward

When we focus on our inner world through quiet reflection, it provides an opportunity to figure out what we are thinking and feeling. It also provides access to our memories, desires, dreams, beliefs, attitudes, values, and hopes. When you open the door to this rich inner world, you can then make decisions about your life that are reflective of your core values. There is no "one right answer," yet there is a decision that will feel right to you when you focus inward. Your inner world is unique to you — like your fingerprint. Let it be your guide.

As I focus on my rich inner world, I let it guide me in the decisions I make for my life.

Gaining Insight

Focusing on our inner world will help us gain insight into ourselves. Insight means deeply understanding our thoughts, feelings, and actions. It means we understand who we are and what makes us tick. We know what works — and what doesn't — so we avoid repeating the same mistakes over and over. Insight provides guidance to help create the lives we desire for the future.

With insight, I gain a deeper understanding of my Self. This Self knowledge helps me create a life I desire going forward.

Finding Your Self

One way of accessing your inner Self is to become aware of the part of you who is the observer — the one who notices, or watches. While there are many ways to do this, one simple exercise is called mindful breathing.

To try this, sit in a comfortable and relaxed position. Close your eyes as you breathe slowly in and out. Bring your attention to the part of you who is aware of the breath flowing in and out. Take a deep breath, relax as you exhale. Ask yourself where you feel the breath the most: nose, chest, abdomen, shoulders? What do you notice in your body? Observe the thoughts that flit in and out. When your attention wanders, which it will, bring it gently back to the breath. Without judgement, embrace whatever comes up. Continue to breathe slowly.

Another way to get in touch with your inner Self is to gaze into your eyes in a mirror and become aware of the "you" who is looking back. Smile or say loving messages to your Self. Notice the thoughts and feelings that arise. Breathe as you do this exercise as well.

These techniques help you learn to stay in the present moment. The present moment is where your inner Self is at its best — calm, loving, and waiting to help.

As I slowly breathe, I am aware of my inner Self. I notice what happens in my body and the thoughts and feelings that come and go. When my attention wanders, I bring my focus back to my breath. I feel calm and centered.

Do It Anyway

Some people say they don't want to look within and get curious about themselves. They hesitate to open their inner door because they are afraid of what they will see. None of us have lived our lives perfectly in the past and we all have parts of ourselves we don't like or feelings we wish would go away. The problem with shutting down these parts and feelings is that it takes *so much energy*. The energy used to shut them down would be better spent exploring gently what is there, repairing the damage we have caused, making amends to those we have hurt, or focusing on doing things differently in the future.

Feel the fear of looking within and do it anyway. This is called courage! When we use compassionate courage to address our fear, we start to grow in new, healthy, and vibrant ways.

*With an open, courageous heart, I look within. I am ready
to grow in new and healthy ways.*

Self Compassion

Because suppressing uncomfortable feelings or parts of ourselves we don't like takes so much energy, we can never truly keep them hidden. They tend to pop out at times when we are under stress, are tired, or otherwise not at our best. Rather than be blindsided by these parts or feelings, it is much better to be honest with ourselves about them. Even though this is difficult, we can practice Self compassion and embrace *all* parts of ourselves.

We often extend compassionate understanding to our friends and loved ones, yet are highly self-critical. For example, when we lose touch with a friend, we might think, "Oh well. He is busy taking care of his parents." But when we think of our own role in not contacting a friend, we tell ourselves what a terrible person we are. Self compassion involves applying the same kindness we extend to others toward ourselves, rather than being judgmental or critical.

When we focus loving-kindness toward ourselves, we begin the process of Self care and forgiving ourselves. Compassionate Self care and forgiveness are the foundation of healing.

I extend the same loving-kindness to my friends and my Self.
I practice Self compassion.

Tending to Your Inner World

Our inner world is constantly changing and needs to do so in response to the changing events of our lives. We need to tend to our inner world, just like we tend to a garden we have planted. Sometimes we plant new seedlings or seeds. At other times, we fertilize, weed, mulch, water or prune depending on weather, soil conditions, and the season.

Within our inner world, we may find parts that aren't serving us well anymore and need to do a little pruning. Other parts might need some nurturing to grow properly. When we look inward, we lovingly tend to ourselves and our inner world in a healthy way. This provides the nurturing attention we need to thrive.

I tend to my inner world as I would to a garden I have planted. I nurture myself in order to grow in a healthy way.

Chapter ❷
How Our Thoughts Can Trip Us Up and What to Do About It

Have you ever said something to yourself like, "I will never get this right, so why bother even trying?" Or, "I'm such an idiot." Our thoughts are very powerful. You might even say they create the world in which we live. Because our brains are so good at thinking, we believe that if we have a thought, it *must* be true. Yet, this is not correct. Our thoughts are often wrong. But when we have been stuck in negative thinking for a long time, it feels normal to us. We don't question the thoughts or slow them down to investigate whether they are based in facts, are pure myth, or fall somewhere in between.

As it happens, thoughts can be observed, questioned, and modified. Learning how to take a step back from your thoughts, strange as it may sound, can actually help you in your journey to reconnect to your Self.

Many books have been written about problematic thoughts, which demonstrates a couple of important points. The first is that this type of thinking causes difficulties for *many* people. It also indicates we may need help to revise them. These thoughts generate negative feelings which in turn cause us to feel bad about ourselves. Then we think more negative thoughts and this becomes a never ending cycle of feeling bad, negative thinking, feeling worse — you get the idea — around and around we go.

In this chapter, we explore specific types of thoughts that get this downward spiral started and provide examples of how they can be changed. When we begin to stop the cycle, we transition into a pattern that is more positive, affirming, and supportive. This new pattern helps support a positive connection to Self.

My thoughts are powerful creators of my world. I am becoming aware
of how my thoughts impact how I feel about my Self.

Noticing and Slowing Down Thoughts

The first step to changing a problematic thought pattern is to simply notice the thought that causes discomfort. These thoughts are critical, demeaning, and cruel. If we spoke the thought out loud to a friend, we wouldn't have many friends. Hurtful thoughts make us feel *less than* — less than adequate, less than capable, less than competent.

Even though it may be uncomfortable, we need to slow down and stay with this thought. Your body reacts to this type of thinking negatively. Imagine calling yourself a nasty name. What do you notice in your body? Does your jaw tighten, palms get sweaty, heart beat faster, face flush, or stomach flip? These physical sensations are messages. They are messages *from* you *to* you — pay attention.

By noticing and acknowledging how our thoughts make us feel, we begin the process of shifting to healthier and more supportive thought patterns.

Just because I think a thought, doesn't make it true. I slow down my thoughts and notice how they influence my feelings.

Questioning Our Thoughts

The next step involves questioning whether the negative thought is true or accurate. As you read through this chapter, begin to have a conversation with yourself about your thoughts. Be gentle and kind as you start this process. Pretend you are asking a friend or respected colleague to clarify something or speak as you would to a child. Questions include:

- Is the thought true? How do I know it's true? Where is proof the thought is true?
- When did this thought first originate? Did someone tell me this? If so, who?
- How do I feel when I believe the thought?
- Would I speak this way to a loved one, family member, friend, or child?
- Was it true at one time, but not any longer?
- If I shared this thought with a trusted friend, what would they say?

Investigating our negative thinking is an important step to having a better relationship with our inner Self because thoughts deeply influence how we feel about ourselves.

With gentle kindness and compassion, I investigate my negative thoughts and explore whether they are true.

Revising Problem Thoughts

Changing our thoughts that are incorrect with accurate and supportive thoughts is the final step. This is often the most difficult part. Because we *believe* our thoughts, it's difficult to see an alternative. But negative thinking is just a bad habit and bad habits can be changed. The remainder of this chapter highlights the most common thought patterns that keep us stuck and includes examples of how to adapt them to be more supportive, accurate, and positive. It may take a little effort and practice, but the improved connection to Self makes this effort well worth it.

I am open to learning how to revise my thoughts to be more accurate, positive, and supportive.

Thought Patterns that Create Disconnection

Nasty Name Calling

Calling ourselves nasty names is unnecessary, demoralizing, and just plain mean. We would never speak to our friends in this way, yet people say the nastiest things to themselves all the time. Examples include: dummy, loser, or lazy. And sadly, there are many more examples out there. Name calling makes us feel bad about ourselves.

When you notice name calling directed toward yourself, slow down and stop. Go back to page 38 and ask yourself the questions listed there. Would you speak this way to your boss, a child, or someone at your church? Speaking gently to yourself is a form of respect. Promise your Self that you will stop name calling. Focus on finding a kinder, gentler, and more compassionate way to address your Self.

When I notice that I'm calling myself a nasty name, I slow down and stop.
I speak to myself as I would to a good friend because I respect my Self.

Perfectionistic Thinking

Perfectionistic thinking is a trap many of us fall into. The words "must" or "should" are often associated with this type of thinking and are used to motivate ourselves or our behavior, but in a negative way.

For example:	Can be changed to:
I must exercise every day.	I exercise as often as I can because I enjoy it.
I should never be late.	I try not to be late, but sometimes the unexpected happens.

It is also used to hold yourself to an impossibly high standard.

For example:	Can be changed to:
I should get all A's.	I study hard so I get the highest grade possible.

Perfectionistic thinking can also involve telling yourself how you "should" or "must" feel when it is not actually how you feel. For example: "I should feel guilty about missing dinner with my mother" can be changed to: "I value spending time with my mother. Having dinner with her supports my values. But I balance this with other priorities in my life."

The result of perfectionistic thinking is that we never measure up. We then feel anxious, guilty, or disappointed in ourselves. No wonder we disconnect from our feelings! Changing these thoughts to reflect what we desire, want, or what supports us, will help us set realistic goals for ourselves. Consequently, we feel more content, positive, and confident.

I change perfectionistic thinking that includes "musts" and "shoulds" to reflect what I desire or like. I then feel more content, positive, and confident and this is supportive of my Self.

Blaming

Blaming causes turmoil and confusion, whether we blame ourselves or others. To tease apart the components of blaming, it is first important to determine which factors are under our control versus the factors under the control of others.

Sometimes we are confused and accept responsibility for events that are *not* under our control. For example: your child gets in a fight at school and you blame yourself, even though you were not there. Conversely, we may try to blame someone else instead of accepting the responsibility that is ours. For example: you strike out playing baseball and you blame the umpire, the sun, or the noisy fans.

Ask yourself, if you took away blame, what problem would be left? Once we define the actual problem, we can then focus our attention and energy on fixing the problem rather than spending our energy on blaming ourselves or others.

I accept responsibility for my thoughts, feelings, and actions. I do not blame myself for others' actions nor do I blame them for mine.

Black and White Thinking

In black and white thinking, every situation is seen on opposite ends of a spectrum with no room for gray areas. A variation of this pattern, called overgeneralizing, happens when we view an isolated incident or event as a never ending, negative pattern. Words to watch out for here include: *always or never, good or bad, all or nothing,* and *success or failure.* This is just another way our thoughts prevent us from feeling good about ourselves.

Examples:	Change to:
I am *bad.*	I behaved poorly.
I *always* mess up.	I made a mistake. I won't repeat it next time.
I'll *never* get it right.	If I make some changes, I'll figure it out.

By recognizing the polarizing words we use, we can revise them to be more realistic, supportive, and empowering for each situation. This, in turn, fosters a positive connection to Self.

I am learning to recognize the pattern of overgeneralizing, and black and white thinking. I change my thoughts to be more realistic and supportive.

Thinking Negatively

Being hyper-focused on the negative events in our lives creates a descending spiral of experience that greatly influences how we feel about ourselves — but not in a good way. For example: Your alarm doesn't go off in the morning making you rush to work. You tell yourself you're having *such a bad day* and thereby set yourself up to *actually* have a bad day. The reality: Yes, it's unpleasant to start the day in a rush. But notice the positives that happen as well. Traffic was light, someone held the door for you, and you arrived at work on time. Negative thinking can ruin your whole day, but by slowing down, noticing the thoughts and changing them, we change how we experience our lives as well.

Some people are so good at negative thinking, every situation becomes a catastrophe. In the above example, if you added: I know I will be late, fired, lose my home, and have to live on the street, it becomes an example of *catastrophic* thinking. This inflames our experience and creates more anxiety than is necessary. We can change our thoughts to be more realistic and soothing: "I can't remember the last time I was late" or "I'll stay a little late tonight to make up my time." Take a couple of deep breaths for good measure.

I view the events in my life in a balanced, realistic way: good and bad things happen. When I notice my thoughts are based in negativity, I modify them to be more accurate and soothing.

Discounting All the Positives

We sometimes discount the positive events in our lives by minimizing our accomplishments or by attributing the good things that happen to luck or happenstance. This is playing small in our lives and it prevents us from feeling positive and confident about ourselves. For example: You receive high marks on a test and tell yourself it was just luck. The reality: You actually studied hard, went to class every day, and took notes, which in turn, resulted in a good grade.

We need to be able to take credit for the effort and the successes we create in our lives. This helps build our Self confidence and a healthy connection with our inner Self.

I take credit for my achievements, accomplishments, and successes in a healthy, realistic way.

Mind Reading

When we mind read, we assume other people are thinking the worst about us without any proof. It includes jumping to conclusions even when we don't have the actual facts. The only way to *really* know what someone is thinking or feeling is to ask them. For example: You arrive at work and your boss is visibly upset. You instantly "know" it is because of something you did wrong and you'll be fired. The reality: Your boss could be upset for any number of reasons that have nothing to do with you. This kind of mind reading and jumping to conclusions takes a huge, negative toll on our emotional well-being.

Sensitivity to others' moods and needs is a sign of empathy. While this is a positive characteristic, mind reading without the facts is exhausting and needlessly puts us on an emotional rollercoaster. The solution is to find out what is going on by asking the other person.

I am not a good mind reader. If I want to know what others
are thinking or feeling, I ask them.

Emotional Reasoning

Thoughts impact and shape our feelings. But if our feelings are caused by the negative and untrue thoughts we've been discussing, then the resulting feeling will also be inaccurate. In other words, *just because we feel a feeling, doesn't make it true.*

If you call yourself a loser (name calling), you will feel sad. Telling yourself "I do the best I can every day," will make you feel better. If you tell yourself the sky is falling (catastrophe), you may feel anxious or afraid. Changing it to "This has been a rough day," changes your feelings to hope or acceptance.

Noticing how our thoughts impact our feelings is an important step to stay connected to our Self.

*I understand my negative thinking impacts how I feel. Changing my
negative thoughts shifts how I feel about my Self.*

Final Thoughts About Problem Thinking

Some of the issues we may experience because of negative thought patterns include: anxiety, low self-esteem, sadness, and anger management problems. Becoming aware of these unsupportive thoughts and changing them will shift how you feel about your Self. Altering the negative thought patterns help us begin to create a more secure, more loving, and more supportive connection with our inner Self.

By noticing my thoughts and their impact on my well-being, I start to create a more secure, loving, and supportive connection to my inner Self.

Chapter ③
You *Can* Change How You Feel

The importance of our emotions and the impact they have on our well-being cannot be over emphasized. Not only is it normal for humans to experience emotions, feelings are part of our navigational system. Emotions give us information, like a GPS, about which direction to turn. In fact, the word emotion comes from Latin meaning to move. Emotions *move* us through life and help us to take action. For example, love and joy move us closer to our loved ones, encouraging us to spend more time with our kids or friends. Anger helps us create firm boundaries. Fear will move us into fight, flight, or freeze mode.

The purpose of emotions is to keep us safe. They have important messages for us. Once we understand our emotions, we realize they *always* make sense. They make sense in a way that is unique to each of us based on our experiences and needs.

But emotions can also cause problems for us and a disconnection from Self, and we will be exploring how that happens in this chapter. Be kind and gentle with yourself. Go slowly — with curiosity and compassion. Breathe. With a better understanding of our amazing emotional system, we can begin to relax and trust our feelings and the messages they have for us.

My emotions provide valuable information about which direction to go or action I should take. I am open to gently exploring them with compassionate curiosity.

Defining Emotions

Our emotional states can be described as a shift away from a neutral, calm state of mind and can be classified in the following way:

Fear: Fear is called an organizing emotion because it is used for survival and takes priority over our other emotions. Fear ranges on a continuum from feeling vaguely worried or anxious through the other end of the spectrum, dread or terror.

Anger: Anger, like our other emotions, is designed to keep us safe as long as we decide on an *appropriate* action to take. Without a thoughtful approach, anger's associated behaviors can push people away or get us into trouble. Annoyance and irritation are examples of low level anger with fury and rage on the high end. Anger can also be a smoke screen for softer underlying emotions like hurt which we will talk about later in this chapter.

Sadness: Sadness ranges from feeling melancholy or disappointed, to despair or anguish. When sadness is temporary, it is a normal part of moving away, letting go, or grieving. But it can also be a message for us to reach out to others for comfort. Sadness should not be confused with depression, of which sadness is one of several other symptoms.

Joy: Perhaps an explanation of a positive emotion like joy doesn't seem necessary, but even joy provides a range of experience from simple pleasure to excitement and wonder. Joy has us move toward or closer to the person or object associated with this feeling.

When our emotions are working properly, they are like the waves on a beach. Though the waves of emotion will vary in size and intensity, one wave always follows another. Without our emotions, life would feel boring and bland. Our feelings allow us to experience and enjoy life in a way that is richer and deeper than if we stayed at a constant, calm neutral. They provide important messages about whether to move closer or away, to set boundaries or make changes. In short, they help us experience our lives to the fullest.

My emotions are constantly changing, like the waves on a beach. They provide a richness of experience so I can enjoy life to the fullest extent possible.

Emotional Pain

Doctors sometimes say that pain is their best friend because it is a message from their patient's body providing clues about what is wrong. In other words, it is pain that helps them locate the problem, make an assessment, formulate a diagnosis, and find an appropriate treatment. If you cut your finger, pain alerts you to the injury so you can determine how deep it is and decide whether it needs a simple bandage or stitches.

Emotional pain serves the same purpose. After an argument with a friend, you might experience a variety of painful emotions: anger, anxiety, or sadness. The emotional pain helps you gauge the depth of the problem, to make a decision about what to do, or what action to take. Do you need to have a talk, apologize, or discontinue the friendship?

Many people try to avoid their emotional pain. They ignore it, distract themselves away from it, self-medicate by drinking or taking drugs, wait for it to disappear or blow over, try to explain it away — really anything to avoid acknowledging or listening to the pain. Yet, as difficult as it may be, we need to listen to our painful emotions. They have valuable messages for us and help us step toward an increased understanding of ourselves.

Emotional pain is my mind's way of alerting me to a problem that needs my attention. Even though this can be difficult, I listen to my emotions to gain understanding of my Self.

Stuck Emotions

One way our emotions cause problems for us is when one particular feeling gets stuck in the on position. For example, fear is exactly what we want to feel for a real threat, like when a bear crosses our path on a hike, because it floods our system with adrenaline and ramps up our breathing and heart rate. But when fear is turned on *all* the time, or we perceive a threat that isn't actually there, we may experience low level anxiety, have sleep problems, or develop physical symptoms like ulcers or panic attacks. Any emotion can become stuck and create problems and discomfort for us. Stuck emotions prevent us from experiencing life to its fullest.

By becoming aware of our stuck emotions, we can start to let them go. Explore your feelings with gentle kindness. How long has the stuck feeling been an issue? When did it originate? Is it appropriate to your actual situation now? Has it always been a problem, or only in certain situations or with specific people? Ask yourself if there are changes you can make in your life that would alleviate this stuck feeling.

The goal is to have greater fluidity of *all* of our emotions so we then make decisions and take actions supportive to our well-being and our inner Self.

As I become aware of my stuck feelings, I do a gentle inquiry to understand and shift them. This is supportive to my Self and my well-being.

Shutting Down

Shutting our emotional system down also causes problems for us. Instead of being stuck on, our emotions can be stuck in the off position. Because feelings can be overwhelming and painful, shutting them down makes sense because it keeps us from feeling the pain. While this works as a short term fix, it doesn't work well as a long term strategy.

For example, if your child is hurt on the playground and you need to rush him to the emergency room, it makes sense to shut down the fear or worry in order to prioritize the action needed, in this case driving to the emergency room safely. But if your emotions stay shut down after returning home, you won't be available to provide the emotional comfort your child needs.

We really only have one emotional switch, so to speak. If we shut one emotion down, it negatively impacts our ability to feel our other emotions as well. And without full access to our emotional guidance system, we have difficulty making decisions, connecting with others and enjoying life. Shutting down our emotions is like losing one of our senses — the music or color is gone from our lives — and we end up feeling empty or flat.

The goal then, is to be aware of the feelings, hear the messages they carry, make the decisions we need to make, take the necessary action, and let them go again. Use your feelings as a means to understand your Self and your needs better.

Shutting my feelings down only works as a short term fix. I am open to the messages my emotions have for me to understand my needs better.

Emotions Are Fast

Another aspect of emotions which creates problems for us is that they happen very fast. They hit with lighting speed. Our response time to feelings is much faster than our response time to thoughts. For example, if we hear a rustling in the bushes next to our hiking trail, we respond quickly to fear and jump away, long before our thoughts catch up to let us know it's just a paper bag rustling in the wind. Responding to our children or significant others from an emotional place, without revisiting to investigate what the quick emotional reaction was all about, can lead us to a disconnection from them — and ourselves.

To understand our feelings better, we must slow down and take some time out to reflect on them. Revisiting the feeling after the emotion has come and gone is how we decipher and make sense of the emotion and come to an understanding of our reaction.

Going back to revisit painful emotions is difficult for many people. After all, if the pain is gone, why not just move on? This may work — for a while. But if we ignore our feelings on a long term basis, we notice that similar emotions or scenarios keep popping up. Like the familiar saying goes, it's like trying to sweep our emotions under the rug. Soon there's so much emotional junk under the rug, we trip over it every time we walk into the room.

It is much better to revisit our feelings, spend time with them, and respond to them on a regular basis. This creates a deeper understanding of ourselves and helps keep us connected to our Self.

I slow down, revisit, and reflect on my feelings to gain a better understanding of my emotions and my Self.

States or Traits

Feelings are states of being, not traits. Our emotions are not who we are. They are a *part* of who we are. People sometimes say things like, "I am lonely" or "I am sad." This takes a temporary feeling or state and makes it into a global statement about who we are. That is overstating things. We can *feel* lonely or we *feel* sad, angry, or happy. We are *more* than just our feelings.

Emotions are constantly changing in response to the events of our lives, just like the waves in the ocean respond to changing weather and wind conditions. Sometimes the waves are gentle and soft: other times, they crash over us. As mentioned earlier, waves constantly ebb and flow and this is similar to how our feelings are constantly changing.

But just as a wave is only a small part of the ocean, our emotions comprise only a small part of us. If we go below the surface of the waves, there is a vast, calm ocean. The ocean represents our inner world which is much more complex, intricate, and multi-faceted than emotions alone.

I am a wonderful human being with a deep, complex, multi-faceted inner world. I am more than my emotions alone.

Surface and Underlying Emotions

Often we are only aware of our surface emotions. Surface emotions serve to get our attention. They also protect or hide our more vulnerable, underlying emotions. For example: Your spouse is late arriving home from work and you are angry (surface emotion). Upon further reflection, you realize you are also anxious because she may have been in a car crash. Or you feel hurt because she didn't take the time to call. Feeling anxious or hurt are the underlying emotions.

We are not always aware of our underlying emotions in the moment because they are obstructed by the surface emotion. To get in touch with what is going on underneath, we need to once again, slow down and look inward. In this example, if you expressed only anger to your spouse, she may accuse you of being unreasonable or overreacting and this could lead to an argument. But if you communicated the underlying emotion of feeling anxious or hurt, your spouse will not only understand you better, she can be more thoughtful about your feelings in the future by phoning or texting when she's running late.

Surface emotions help us become aware of a problem. Understanding our underlying emotions and how they fuel our reactive surface emotions leads us to a greater comprehension of our needs. With this awareness, we can then communicate our deeper, vulnerable feelings and needs to our loved ones. In turn, they can respond to us in a way that works for us and for our relationship.

When I understand both my surface and underlying emotions, I gain insight into my Self and can communicate my needs better to others.

Sore Spots

Sore spots are emotional wounds that are so sensitive that when someone or something bumps one, we go ballistic. If emotions serve to get our attention to a problem, a sore spot does so in a big way. A sore spot exists because something in the present moment reminds you of a painful way you felt in the past. It's an old wound that hasn't healed properly.

A good indication a sore spot has been bumped is when we find ourselves overreacting to a relatively small event. Let's use the previous example of feeling upset when your spouse is late coming home from work. As you slow down and reflect on the feelings that arise, in this case anger, anxiety, or hurt, a memory comes to you. You are waiting alone at your middle school: everyone else has left. Your father was supposed to pick you up but he was often unreliable, late, or sometimes forgot entirely. At the time, you felt frustrated, scared, sad, abandoned, and powerless. This is your sore spot. When your spouse is late, your old childhood feelings get triggered.

When working through a sore spot, it can be helpful to remind ourselves that we are not the same person now as we were when the original event happened. In our example, an adult has skills and power that children don't possess. So, even though the feelings you had back in middle school are still as real as ever, they don't really fit your current situation. By starting a gentle, compassionate inquiry into the images and memories that arise, we gain a new understanding of these old hurts. Slowly, we begin to heal our old emotional wounds in our current relationships and with ourselves.

I am becoming aware of my sore spots and old emotional wounds. I reflect on where they came from so that I understand my Self and heal in the present moment.

Conflicting Feelings

We can have more than one feeling at the same time. The saying, "I'm of two minds" is a common reference to this. For example, a college student who is leaving home to study in another city may have the mixed feelings of excitement for a new adventure, anxiety about living in a new place on their own, and sadness to be leaving family and friends behind. Which feeling gets attention first? What action should we take? Because of the emotional discomfort, we might attempt to push one or more of the feelings aside, yell at ourselves to get over it, or suppress the feelings. Yet, this doesn't work very well.

When we acknowledge our conflicting feelings, we have an opportunity to learn more about ourselves. We can give each feeling a voice. In the example above, listening to the fear provides an opportunity to plan well in advance for things like finding a place to live, purchasing food plans, or to simply remind ourselves we are resourceful and competent. By listening to the sadness over leaving friends and family, we put a plan in place for having people come to visit, going home for the holidays, or keeping in contact via social media.

Understanding our conflicting emotions provides an opportunity to take care of all parts of ourselves. Our feelings always make sense when we take time to know and understand them.

When I have conflicting emotions, I focus on each of them in turn and listen to their messages. I learn about my Self and my needs.

Stuffing our Feelings

How many times are boys told "don't cry," or "be a man"? How many times are girls criticized for being "overly dramatic"? It is no wonder we learn to suppress our feelings — and at an early age. When the door to our feelings has been shut for a very long time, we worry if we open the door, we won't be able to handle them or we will be totally overwhelmed. We worry that the crying will never stop or the anger will overtake us. Conversely, we may tell ourselves that our emotions don't have *any* value so there is no sense in paying attention to them.

The process of pushing our feelings down is like cooking a pot of soup on the stove. The vegetables of the soup (feelings) are in the bottom of the pot. When life turns up the heat and the cover of the pot is on, the soup and vegetables will boil over. But when we take off the lid periodically and let the steam escape, the pressure is relieved. Acknowledging and validating our emotions by talking with others about them, helps relieve the emotional pressure. If we have been stuffing feelings for a long time, we may want or need some help with this. Talking with professionals, therapists, friends, clergy, or wise family members can be very helpful.

Remember, the feelings themselves are *normal*. Suppressing feelings keeps us numbed out and disconnected. Accepting all of our emotions helps us understand ourselves better and this understanding creates a better connection with our Self.

I no longer stuff my feelings. I gently embrace them and ask for help when I need it. By doing so, I create a better relationship with my Self.

Distractions and Numbing

Using distractions and numbing is a little different from stuffing our feelings because we look for something outside ourselves to reduce the emotional pressure. The distractions we use are diverse: spending hours on the computer, shopping excessively, eating compulsively, watching TV endlessly, using alcohol or drugs, working, sleeping, or exercising all the time — the list goes on and on.

Overuse of distractions can quickly work against us. Eating a whole pizza may help us temporarily forget how much we dislike our job, but the weight gain, increased cholesterol, and lowered self-esteem do not help us feel good about ourselves. An occasional glass of wine may be enjoyable, but when the glass turns into a bottle, or you can't relax without a drink, it is important to take a look at the behavior and the hidden underlying emotions.

Numbing strategies help us avoid painful feelings, which makes perfect sense, in the short term. As we let go of the dysfunctional behaviors, our painful feelings will become more apparent. We may need assistance with this process, especially if the behaviors have been going on for a long time. Contacting friends, 12-Step groups, therapists, or other professionals may be helpful.

When we remove the distractions and gently reflect inward, we start to understand our feelings and know ourselves better. We won't need to use the numbing or distracting behaviors once we have created a healthier, solid connection with our inner Self.

As I start to understand the reasons for the numbing and distracting behaviors I use, I let them go and open myself to a healthier connection with my Self.

Chapter ④
Tips for Repairing Other Disconnects in Our Lives

There are other ways we disconnect from our Self. Some prevent us from connecting in a healthy way while others simply keep the disconnection going.

Roles

Roles are assigned growing up and serve to keep a family in balance. Their purpose is to compensate for dysfunction in the family, like addiction or mental health issues. Roles are part of the unwritten rules of a family and most often, are not conscious. The positive aspect of roles is that they provide a child a means to survive difficult family dynamics. But they can also cause confusion and pain because they lock us into a set of behaviors that are constricting or confining, or they keep us in a role that is no longer necessary or needed.

There are several common roles found in families. The "clown" tells jokes and funny stories which lightens the mood in an otherwise tense home. Underneath, the family clown often feels scared or inadequate. Another is the "perfect child," who focuses on others' needs but denies their own. The "black sheep" uses acting out behavior to distract attention away from the other problems in the family, but is an underachiever. The "chameleon" is laid back and quiet, but doesn't initiate or make decisions and is often lonely. Finally, the "family champion" is disciplined and organized, yet is inflexible and has a great fear of making mistakes.

Childhood roles are a template for how we act in later relationships and cause problems until we become conscious of them. Once we are aware of the impact of the roles we adopted, we can decide whether we want to keep the role, change it, or discard it altogether. Consciously choosing and embracing our roles helps us reconnect with our inner Self.

As I become aware of the role I play in my life, I consciously decide whether I want to keep, change, or discard the role altogether.

Stories We Tell Ourselves

The stories we tell ourselves help weave our life events together so we can make sense of them and create a coherent narrative. Yet, many times the stories told are not true. Stories that create difficulties for us include: not measuring up to someone else's expectations, looking at only one aspect of ourselves, or stories that were true at some point in the past, but are no longer true.

For example, let's say you struggled in school and received poor grades. The story told by your family and teachers was that you never finished your homework — you were just not academically inclined. If you believed this story, you might not apply yourself in school — what's the use? Why even try? In reality, you were a high energy kid who needed lots of exercise, a structured, quiet study place, and a sugar free diet to help you focus. Thus the story is changed. You weren't lazy or stupid. You were a child with specific needs that weren't met with understanding. The new story is healthy and adaptive rather than negative and demeaning.

It is never too late to challenge and change these old stories. In fact, even if the old story can't be changed, we are the authors of our lives now and it is never too late to alter the future outcome of our story. We can go back to page 38 where we learned to question our thoughts and substitute the word story for thought. Go within and inquire whether the story told about your Self is actually true.

I listen to the story I tell myself, question whether it's true, and notice how I feel when I tell this story. I am the author of my life and my story.

Identifying the Problem Correctly

Sometimes people believe that they are the problem. We may have been blamed so often by family or spouses that this idea becomes internalized. But this just isn't true. *The problem is always the problem.*

You may be a person with a problem (or problems). You may have had the problem for a long time. You may not know what to do about the problem. Your family, friends, or spouse may not like the particular problem you have. But you are just an imperfect person, like the rest of us, doing the best you can. When we correctly identify the *actual* problem, we can then start working to find solutions and make the changes needed.

It is impossible to have a good, healthy connection with your Self if you think *you* are the problem. But by correctly identifying that you are a *person with a problem,* you start to improve your connection to Self.

I may be a person with a problem, but I am not the problem.

Themes

We may have underlying, negative themes that fuel a disconnection from our inner selves as well. Themes are learned, negative beliefs about ourselves and impact us on a very deep level. They are like music playing just under our conscious awareness and set the tone for many of our relationships, activities, and feelings.

Examples of negative themes include: I'm not good enough, I'm not lovable, I can't trust myself, I am weak, or I am a failure. These themes often begin in childhood and are a child's explanation of a complex and confusing world in which we lacked life experience and support.

For example, children often assume negative events are caused by them. If mom was depressed, the child's explanation of mommy's bad mood is: I'm bad, I'm not lovable, or I'm not good enough. Over time, this theme is globally applied to other relationships and circumstances. As adults, even in new relationships, we unconsciously play the old themes that reinforce the deeply held, erroneous belief.

These themes keep us feeling bad and disconnected from who we really are. So, just as we explored our thoughts, feelings and stories, we can also examine where these themes originated by asking ourselves where we learned the belief and whether it is still true now. Once we are aware of the negative theme, it can be revised to more adaptive and positive themes: I am good enough, I am lovable, I can trust myself, I'm strong, I am successful. We adopt themes that reflect who we truly are, support our well-being, and nurture a good connection to Self.

As I gain awareness of an underlying theme in my life, I discard what is no longer true or helpful. I adopt a new theme that supports my happiness and well-being.

Core Issue

Another way of talking about a negative theme is to say it is our core issue. There are several ways we can recognize when a negative theme or core issue has been triggered. Sometimes there is a familiar, déjà vu feeling to it. Other times, memories or images from old hurts and wounds arise in the present moment, even though the current situation is different. You may have a sense that you have "heard it before," or it's the same old feeling coming up — again. Life has a way of bringing these core issues to our attention over and over until they're healed. Remember, pain tells us there is a problem that needs our attention.

Here is a little story to help make sense of this concept. Imagine hiking up a mountain on a circular path, around and around as we go higher. When we start our hike, we can barely see through the trees — is that a lake (aka: core issue) we see? We can't be sure, because our view is obstructed. As we continue our hike up the mountain, we eventually arrive at the same spot. Because of the higher elevation, we can *definitely* see it's a lake. As we hike higher, we gain a new viewpoint. Each time we revisit our core issue, we see it from a new perspective. Seeing our core issue from a new perspective allows us to heal a little deeper.

Revisiting these past hurts, negative themes, and core issues is an opportunity to heal them in the present moment, creating a greater understanding and reconnection with your Self.

I am curious about my core issue. When it comes around again, I know this is an opportunity to heal an old wound in the present moment.

Coping Strategies

There is a saying that if the only tool we have in our tool belt is a hammer, then every problem better be a nail. Coping strategies are the tools we use to handle the stressors of life and to keep us feeling emotionally safe. Most of the strategies we use are neutral, in and of themselves. Some of the things we have talked about like shutting down, using distractions, numbing out, or assuming a role are actually coping strategies. But overusing a *single* strategy, using a tool that has negative consequences, or not being conscious about the tools we use, creates imbalance and disconnection in our lives.

Let's take shopping, for example. A little "retail therapy" can help lift our mood by providing a distraction away from a stressful day at work. Yet if used habitually, it can lead to overwhelming debt. It may also prevent us from doing the soul searching necessary to determine whether it is time to look for a new job or career.

To stay connected with ourselves, we need to have *multiple* tools in our tool belt. Some of these include: practicing self-care, meditation or prayer, talking with a friend, listening to music, playing with your cat, exercise, writing a gratitude journal, and more. The more tools in our tool belt, the more flexibility we have available in response to stressful situations. This is called resiliency and resiliency is a sign of health.

I am conscious of the strategies I use to cope with life's stressors. I am willing to obtain new tools to help me. This is a sign of strength and resiliency.

What We Think Versus What Others Think

We can lose the connection with ourselves by overly focusing on what others think. We all need input from our loved ones from time to time because we gain valuable insight and a fresh perspective from them. While the decisions you make will have an impact on people in your life, no one else has to actually live with the decisions and choices made but *you*. It's important to filter the advice received from others carefully to be sure you live according to your *own* inner guide.

If we give too much weight to others' ideas and opinions, we end up confused. Consulting with people whose opinions we value or who have more life experience and knowledge should be used as a way to gather information. This valuable information can then be used to make your *own* decisions. Go within and access your inner Self. Practice trusting your Self as a guide to your desires, dreams, and goals.

*I listen to others' advice, but I live according to my inner
Self's goals, dreams, and desires.*

Mistakes and Growth

Making mistakes is part of life and part of being human. In fact, we need to give ourselves *permission* to make some mistakes. Think about learning to ride a bike. Making mistakes was simply a part of the learning process. By falling over, we not only learned complex balancing skills, but also persistence. Mastering something difficult builds Self esteem and Self confidence.

Sometimes we spend too much energy beating ourselves up for making a mistake. Or we focus so long and hard on the mistake itself that we forget to look for the *lesson* we can learn from it.

Admitting we made a mistake takes courage. Learning from our mistakes — *this is growth!* By staying curious and open about our mistakes, we stay connected with our inner Self.

Mistakes are simply an opportunity for growth.

Chapter **5**
Continuing the Connection

You may have discovered a few hidden treasures that speak to you in these chapters: negative thoughts that have become a habit, feelings that cause you problems, or some patterns or themes you'd like to modify. You may have initiated positive changes with these already. But how do we make *lasting* changes, have a good relationship with ourselves, and maintain a safe and secure connection to Self?

Practice. Practice. Practice.

Connecting to your Self is not something you do once. It is a *practice* of constantly returning to your core, looking within, and checking in with your inner Self. The more you practice, the more you will trust the knowledge already in your possession. You are not the same person today as you were yesterday. You will be slightly different tomorrow. It makes sense to spend time with your Self regularly.

Some people use prayer or meditation to help guide them to this inner connection. Others spend time in nature. Find spare moments in your daily life to tune in, like waiting for a traffic light to change or for the water to boil for your tea. Return to the photos and reflections in this book to help remind you of your new-found insights. There is no right or wrong way to do this. Just know that practice is the key to unlocking and staying connected to your inner Self.

I practice looking inward daily and delight in the discovery of my Self.

Practice Honesty

It can be difficult to admit to ourselves our true, deep, inner feelings. Being honest with ourselves is a form of Self respect. Being honest with others shows we respect them. Honesty is one of the ways we demonstrate love toward Self and others. To maintain a connection with our inner Self, we must practice honesty.

Out of respect for my Self and others, I practice honesty.

Practice Making Changes

Sailors often talk about making a course correction. With sailing, the wind and ocean conditions are constantly changing. To stay on course and reach the desired destination, many small adjustments must be made at the helm and to the sails. And so it is with our lives. Life brings many surprises and changes and we will constantly need to make adjustments. The more connected we are to our inner Self, the easier it becomes to make our own small course corrections going forward.

I practice making changes and adjustments in my life as I move forward.

Practice Doing What Works — For You

We can get ready for an occasional bad day by preparing a list of healthy actions to take or people to contact that we know from past experience help us cope or shift our mood. This awareness and insight into what works for *you* is Self knowledge and Self care at its best. For those dealing with persistent sadness, it may help to light a candle, take the dog for a walk, or call a friend on the phone. For anxiety, taking a swim, a bubble bath, or watching a funny movie can be a healthy distraction. For anger, cooling off by hitting a punching bag, or taking several long, slow breaths may be helpful. Other ideas include journaling, working out, going to a museum, signing up for a class, cooking a healthy meal, taking a nap, or spending time in nature.

The specific struggles we experience are as different and unique as the solutions we implement to overcome them. Yet knowing ahead of time what helps *you* cope and then practicing *what works for you* is an important part of maintaining a healthy connection to your inner Self.

I practice doing what works for me by preparing a healthy coping plan ahead of time so I'm ready if a bad day strikes.

Practice Asking for Help

Asking other people for help is not only OK, it is a sign of strength. Not one of us gets through life all on our own. Loneliness and a sense of isolation can give us the incorrect impression that no one will understand or that talking about things won't help or change anything. *This is absolutely not true.* Loneliness and isolation are the enemies of healing. Biologically, our brains are wired from birth to have connection with others. Creating a connection with ourselves and creating healthy, empathic, and supportive connections with others go hand in hand.

There are always people available to help, whether it's friends, family, neighbors, clergy, doctors, 12-Step programs, or therapists. Many times we need to connect with others who are kind and nurturing to help normalize what we feel and experience before we can truly connect with and embrace our inner Self. We are stronger and better together.

I reach out to supportive others when I feel stuck, isolated,
or alone knowing this is a sign of strength.

Practice Laughter

A good belly laugh is great medicine. It releases endorphins, our feel good hormones. It is important not to take ourselves too seriously. Watch old sitcoms on TV, read the comics in the paper, or watch some funny YouTube videos. See the humor in life — in ourselves, in others and in the world around us. Life is short. Enjoy it!

I practice laughter every day.

Practice Being Your Own Best Friend

If we think of ourselves as a cherished friend, many of our inner struggles go away. Though many find this difficult to get started, one way to do this is to make a list of qualities you like about yourself and read it every day. Start with five items and add at least one more every day. Ask a trusted friend or loved one to help you if this is too hard for you.

Practicing a version of a loving-kindness meditation is another way to start your friendship with your Self. Here is one that is short and simple to remember:

> May I be peaceful,
> May my heart stay open,
> May I remember the beauty of my true Self,
> May my fullest potential be realized,
> May I be healed.

Practice empathy and Self compassion daily.

From this moment forward, I am my own best friend and
I practice empathy and Self compassion.

Practice Loving Yourself

Love is an action word. What can you do today to show how much you love yourself? Put your needs at the top of the list. It may mean saying no to the new community fund raising project. Or, it could mean taking a nap in the middle of the day. Every day will be different. But loving yourself is a prerequisite to having a good relationship and connection to Self. It says: I'm important. I matter. I am special.

I practice loving myself every day. I am important. I matter. I am special.

Practice Reconnecting to Self

The world is filled with wonder and our lives can be too. Each moment is quickly gone and the next moment brings something new. When we are connected to our inner Self — when we really know who we are — we can handle each new and precious moment with confidence, ease and enjoyment. When we do life right, growth is a process that continues throughout our lives. We are never finished. Delight in your growth and transformation. Have an amazing journey through life. Enjoy a wonderful connection to your Self.

*I delight in my growth. I embrace my amazing journey and
a wonderful connection to Self.*

Photography Notes & Locations

All photos were taken by Dave Merrill with a Nikon D5100,
with lenses ranging from 10 mm to 500 mm.

Photography As Meditation

My practice of photography is part of a walking and resting meditation. This process uses the power of the mind to heal itself, while having unexpected encounters with the natural world. For more on my approach to photography, or to purchase fine art prints, visit: www.DaveMerrillPhotography.com.

Photo Locations

Cover Photo: Hibiscus Flower | Edmonds, WA
11) Morning Glory | Queen Anne Hill, Seattle, WA
13) Foggy Path | Vashon Island, WA
15) Stepping Stones | Daitokuji Temple, Kyoto, Japan
17) Dove of Peace | Nagasaki, Japan
19) Beach Light | West Seattle, WA
21) Tulips | Fir Island, WA
23) Plum Blossom | West Seattle, WA
25) Translucence | Woodland Park Rose Garden, Seattle, WA
27) The Candle | Seattle Japanese Garden, Seattle, WA
29) Vibrant Trail | Maui, HI
31) Luminous | Woodland Park Rose Garden, Seattle, WA
33) Sunflower | Edmonds, WA
35) Amida Buddha | Kamakura, Japan
37) Prayer Flags | Dzogchen Retreat Center USA, Eugene, OR
39) Tree Trunks | Montana de Oro State Park, CA
41) Madrona Tree | Richmond Beach, WA
43) Matcha | Mt Koya San, Japan
45) Garden Steps | Kamakura, Japan
47) Sky-Clouds | Sedona, AZ
49) Sunset | Marina, CA
51) Shell | West Seattle, WA
53) Sun in Hand | Richmond Beach, WA
55) Jeep Sunset | Seattle, WA
57) Beach Clouds | West Seattle, WA
59) River Prayer | Maui, HI
61) Forest Path | Vashon Island, WA
63) Marina Beach | Marina, CA

65) Purple Rose | Woodland Park Rose Garden, Seattle, WA
67) Orchid | Edmonds, WA
69) Roses | Woodland Park Rose Garden, Seattle, WA
71) Sand Garden | Tofukuji Temple, Kyoto, Japan
73) Beach Impression | Marina, CA
75) Reflections | Seattle Japanese Garden, Seattle, WA
77) Hydrangea | Itoshima, Japan
79) Water Drops | Edmonds, WA
81) Wedded Rocks | Itoshima, Japan
83) Iris | Seattle Japanese Garden, Seattle, WA
85) Solo Hiker | Maui, HI
87) Moss Garden | Saiho-ji Temple, Kyoto, Japan
89) Beach Bubbles | Edmonds, WA
91) Bamboo | Seattle Chinese Garden, West Seattle, WA
93) Mt Rainier Moonrise | Maury Island, WA
95) Koinobori | Iyashi no Sato, Japan
97) Everyday Buddha | Sakya Monastery, Seattle, WA
99) Double Sunflowers | West Seattle, WA
101) Tulips II | Fir Island, WA
103) Mt. Fuji | Lake Kawaguchiko, Japan
105) Sailboat | West Seattle, WA
107) Madrona Tree II | Richmond Beach, WA
109) Roses | Woodland Park Rose Garden, Seattle, WA
111) Lucky Cat | Ise, Japan
113) Open Arms | Cambria, CA
115) Hibiscus | Edmonds, WA
117) Closer Look | Woodland Park Rose Garden, Seattle, WA

About the Author & Photographer

Susan K. Merrill is a Licensed Marriage and Family Therapist in private practice in Orange County, California. Susan has a masters degree in Counseling Psychology and specializes in the treatment of trauma using Eye Movement Desensitization and Reprocessing (EMDR) and couples counseling using Emotionally Focused Therapy (EFT). Before becoming a therapist, she worked as a massage therapist, insurance underwriter, and airline employee. She has lived in three countries on three different continents. Her own journey to "reconnect to self" is on-going. Susan shares her life with her husband and two amazing cats. When she is not working, writing, or sailing, she is likely traveling.

Dave Merrill's love of nature and meditation inspires his *Healing Image Photography*. He has had a great passion for photography from an early age. Dave teaches alternative healing practices centered on breath and awareness in the Seattle area. His beautiful images capture the healing power of the present moment. Dave enjoys looking deeply at the world, soaking in hot springs, and travel — whether to the back yard or around the world.